PTERODACTYL

by Harold T. Rober

BUMBA BOOKS™

LERNER PUBLICATIONS ◆ MINNEAPOLIS

Note to Educators:

Throughout this book, you'll find critical thinking questions. These can be used to engage young readers in thinking critically about the topic and in using the text and photos to do so.

Lerner Publications Company
A division of Lerner Publishing Group, Inc.
241 First Avenue North
Minneapolis, MN 55401 USA

For reading levels and more information, look up this title at www.lernerbooks.com.

Library of Congress Cataloging-in-Publication Data

Names: Rober, Harold T.
Title: Pterodactyl / by Harold T. Rober.
Description: Minneapolis : Lerner Publications, [2017] | Series: Bumba books. Dinosaurs and prehistoric beasts | Audience: Age 4–8. | Audience: K to grade 3. | Includes bibliographical references and index.
Identifiers: LCCN 2016018694 (print) | LCCN 2016023329 (ebook) | ISBN 9781512426397 (lb : alk. paper) | ISBN 9781512429060 (pb : alk. paper) | ISBN 9781512427349 (eb pdf)
Subjects: LCSH: Pterodactyls—Juvenile literature. | Dinosaurs—Juvenile literature.
Classification: LCC QE862.P7 R6225 2017 (print) | LCC QE862.P7 (ebook) | DDC 567.918—dc23

LC record available at https://lccn.loc.gov/2016018694

Manufactured in the United States of America
1 – VP – 12/31/16

LERNER
SOURCE

Expand learning beyond the printed book. Download free, complementary educational resources for this book from our website, www.lerneresource.com.

Table of Contents

Pterodactyl Flew

Pterodactyl was a flying reptile.

It lived millions of years ago.

It is extinct.

Pterodactyl was not a dinosaur.

But it lived at the same time as dinosaurs.

Do you know the names of any dinosaurs?

Pterodactyl was the size

of a chicken.

People have found fossils

of flying reptiles.

Fossils tell us how big

an animal was.

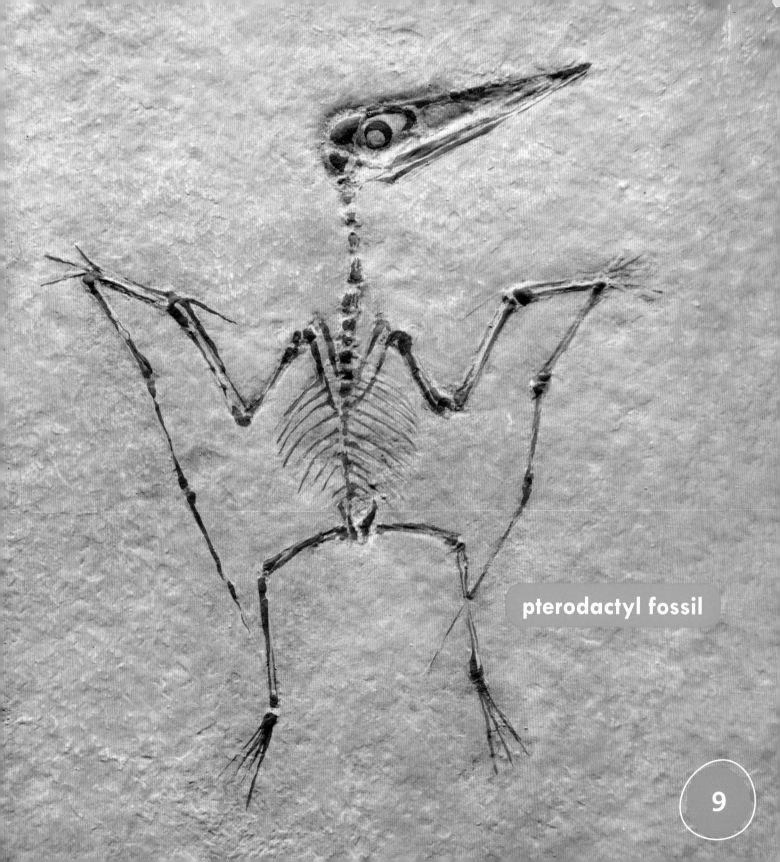

pterodactyl fossil

9

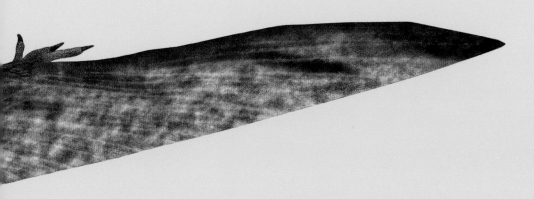

Flying reptiles had wings.

The wings were made of skin.

This skin stretched from the arms
to the legs.

Flying reptiles had long beaks.

They scooped up fish with

their beaks.

They ate other small animals too.

Many flying reptiles had crests on their heads.

Some crests were large.

Others were small.

Why do you think flying reptiles had crests on their heads?

Sometimes these animals walked on the ground.

They walked on all four legs.

Flying reptiles

made nests.

They laid their eggs

in the nests.

Most flying reptiles lived in groups.

These groups were called flocks.

Do you know any other animals that live in flocks?

Parts of a Pterodactyl

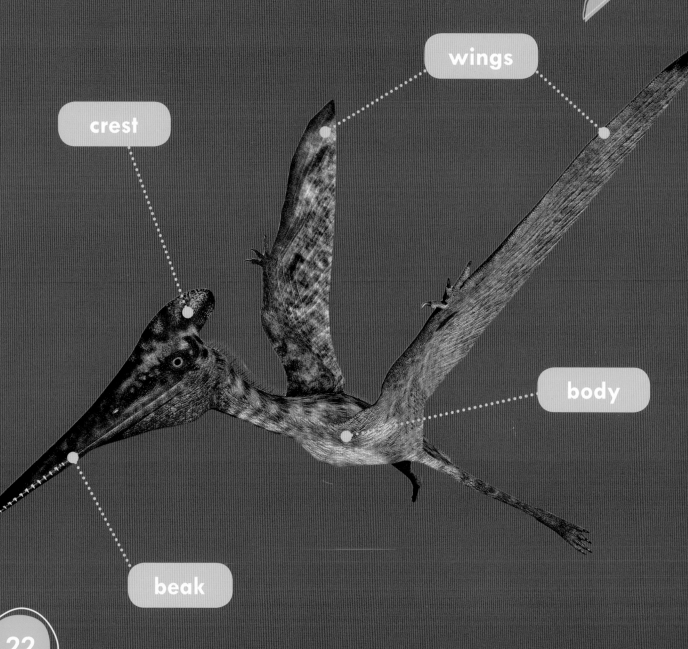

crest

wings

body

beak

Picture Glossary

beaks

hard mouths
that stick out

crests

hard shapes on
top of the head

extinct

no longer alive

fossils

bones or other pieces
of an animal from
long ago that has
turned to rock

Index

Read More

Alpert, Barbara. *Pterodactyl.* Mankato, MN: Amicus High Interest, 2014.

Legendre, Philippe. *I Can Draw!: Dinosaurs, Dragons, and Prehistoric Creatures.* Irvine, CA: Walter Foster Publishing, 2015.

Rober, Harold T. *Triceratops.* Minneapolis: Lerner Publications, 2017.

Photo Credits